Author Marketing
PLAYBOOK
#1

*Using Your Words for Marketing,
Hooking the RIGHT Book Buyers,
and Growing Audience*

DEBORAH RILEY-MAGNUS

AUTHOR MARKETING PLAYBOOK #1

*Using Your Words for Marketing,
Hooking the RIGHT Book Buyers,
and Growing Audience*

DEBORAH RILEY-MAGNUS

Published by Little Pen Press

Copyright © 2017 Deborah Riley-Magnus
All rights reserved.

ISBN-10: 1976296099

ISBN-13: 978-976296093

Without limiting the rights under copyright reserved above, no part of this publication may be reproduced, stored, or transmitted in any form or by any means, without prior written permission of both the copyright owner and the above publisher of this book.

CONTENTS

Introduction	Page 1
Mastering Marketing	Page 5
What is Marketing?	Page 7

LESSON ONE: Using Your Words for Marketing Success — Page 9
- Short Power Pitches — Page 11
- Sound Bites that Bite Harder — Page 21
- Locating Your Query Targets — Page 31
- Synopsis, Blurbs, and Pitch Power — Page 35
- The Perfect Query for Every Need — Page 41

LESSON TWO: Hooking Book Buyers — Page 63
- Locating Unique Hooks — Page 65
- Identifying YOUR audience — Page 73
- Audience Expansion - ©SuperGenre Techniques — Page 85
- Being Genuine and Making Connections! — Page 95

LESSON THREE: Growing Audience — Page 99
- Platforms that Work Hard — Page 105
- Cross Marketing Concepts — Page 119
- Platform Expansion — Page 125
- Multi-Level Marketing — Page 133
- Marketing Time Management — Page 139

INTRODUCTION

Isn't it amazing how a writer can sit and type thousands of words, but never find the right words to market what they've written? We've all been there. Remember the first time someone asked you what your book was about? How your mouth went dry and your brain slammed to a screeching halt? We feel like we've been unfairly put on a spot, so we bumble our way through, spouting scenes, and character names, and random plot points. Wow, maybe we should have been prepared?

It's not unusual, most authors are in the same leaking boat, but learning how to use our words for marketing success is as simple and creative as writing that wonderful book. Understanding how to connect with powerful audiences and turn them into loyal fans isn't complex at all. Building bigger and bigger fan base is easier than you think. It's all done the same way you wrote the book—with creative thinking and wonderful word choices.

Oh, and a little planning, too.

That's why we're here. Welcome to the ***Author Marketing Playbook #1, Using Your Words for Marketing, Hooking the Right Book Buyers, and Growing Audience***. Notice these are PLAYBOOKS, and not workbooks. It's because we play when we create, and that's the most effective approach to marketing. This playbook will set the foundation for smart and entertaining marketing that, with follow-through and consistency, can carry you to the best seller list.

We will cover the unusual, and unbelievably obvious, approaches to marketing that seemed to have been hiding all our author lives. We'll explore platforms, cross marketing, and cover the most important thing for really good marketing—marketing time management! *Author Marketing Playbook #1* is the first giant step toward book sales success.

Author Marketing Success Playbook #2 covers charities, the media, the most powerful way to use social networking, and magical ways to keep your marketing momentum alive. It will explore new, creative ways to reach more audiences, and it explains how to build your author career with a great plan. It also explains ways to analyze successful promotions and build on those successes.

Author Marketing Playbook #3 takes a writer to the final elements of truly successful author career—writing for the market. Imagine choosing your audience before you create the story? Imaging knowing how responsive and ready that audience is for your coming book? It's all available for the taking, and when a writer is seeking sales success, like any other business person in the world, it's wisest to listen to the market and ride the wave.

These playbooks describe techniques, show examples, then invite you to play and create as many variations and directions as your specific book unique hook elements can take you. When you play with the assignments, be silly, be foolish, be as creative as when writing your books. Don't worry about whether it will work or if anyone has tried it before. As the lessons fall into place, you will instinctively learn what can work, what will work, what's worth the risk, and what isn't practical.

We are creative people. Be playful with your marketing. It will take the stinging fear of marketing away, and open so many doors you'll be excited to walk through them all. Smile and know that the journey you're about to embark upon is an exciting expedition most of your competition never even tries. Leave other authors behind in the dust and market your way to real sales success!

MASTERING MARKETING

Mastery comes with time and practice. Polishing writing skills is nothing new to authors, but when it comes to marketing, they tend to wonder which way to run—AWAY. They may think it's a right brain/left brain issue. They probably worry that it's a time suck. Worst of all, after trying ineffective marketing techniques—doing those techniques with all their other author friends, all shouting at the same book buyer at the same time—they most likely feel that marketing just doesn't work.

Marketing does work. What they're doing isn't marketing.

Real marketing efforts never lump together with the competition and hope for sales. Do you really think Mars Candies hangs out with Hershey's Chocolates on Twitter and shares marketing strategies? Of course not. They also don't share their customers with the competition in hopes of getting more customers, or do the exact same promotion all the other candy companies are doing, thinking it will work.

Why? Because it doesn't work and it's not good business. It's time for smart authors to realize that their book is their product. As a business trying to sell its product, it's time to start thinking like a real business. With that, everything changes!

WHAT IS MARKETING?

The best way to answer this question is to start with what marketing isn't.

Marketing IS NOT publicity. Publicity is an entirely different arena that involves the media, the press, and various approaches to charities.

Marketing IS NOT promotion. Promotion includes advertising and promotional items, all costing money, sometimes a lot of money.

Marketing, however, is something very different and extremely powerful for creating sales, no matter what your product is. Marketing isn't expensive, and in many cases, can be done without spending a nickel.

Marketing is creating awareness. Let me repeat that a little louder. MARKETING IS CREATING AWARENESS. Awareness for your book, the unique elements inside your book that targeted audiences will relate to, and awareness of you, the author, who wrote a book loaded with things the audience loves. Creating awareness isn't shouting, "Buy my book!" over and over again. Creating awareness is sharing posts about dogs to dog lovers because your book has a wonderful dog character that drives the story. Creating awareness is sharing cooking tips because your main character is a foodie and you've connected with groups of people who love to cook and eat.

Creating awareness is finding the common ground upon which you and your book can build a loyal fan base. Marketing is saying things your target audience wants to hear, not telling them what you want them to do—buy your book. Marketing is the subtle push that is the primary difference between trying to sell, and allowing people to buy. Marketing is nothing short of magic, but to be this kind of book selling wizard, you need to see marketing for what it is. Creating awareness and connections.

Powerful marketing has to do with what you say, how you say it, where you say it, when you say it, and most importantly, always being entertaining and/or informative along the way.

Let's jump right into the pool!

LESSON ONE
USING YOUR WORDS FOR MARKETING SUCCESS

Remember when that person asked what your book was about? This time you're going to have the answer. Whether it's a friend, a stranger, a literary agent, publisher, book seller, or unique location for a book signing event, you will not only have the perfect answer to that question, you'll know it by heart.

Using your words effectively when talking business about your book is vital. It tells the listener that:

- You write well
- You know your story intimately
- You understand the important elements of the book and how it relates to your target audience
- And that you are a professional

Armed with that kind of tool, you can't lose.

Too many authors slap together a standard query letter, or press release, or event request and copy/paste it off to everyone and anyone. That's not using your words well. That's trying to run away from the task by making it as easy and quick as possible. Good marketing takes a little more time and attention to detail.

Real marketing is connecting with an audience, and sometimes that's a book buyer. Sometimes that audience is a publisher, or an agent, or a reporter, or the owner of a location you know will be great for your book signing event. Using your words carefully and crafting the perfect message can make or break a query, or event, or even a possibly profitable sales relationship.

Unfortunately, there are no short cuts for doing this well. You can become very savvy and astute at it and that does save time, but using short cuts only tells the receiver of the message that you didn't care enough to do it well. Don't be *that* author! Be the one that dazzles them and makes them want to represent you, or publish your book, or report on your event, or have you in their shop to sign books. We all know that words are power. It's time to use them for marketing power.

SHORT POWER PITCHES

Why do you need a short power pitch for your book? Some call it a 25-word pitch and others call it an elevator pitch, but the real question is…why do YOU need one? Maybe you already have an agent or publisher. Maybe you skipped that step altogether and self-published. Either way, you still need a short power pitch. You need them for:

- Queries—and a query is for far more then querying a literary agent
- Book and Back Cover Blurbs
- Synopsis
- Press Releases
- Easy Twitter Posts
- Limited Posts for Promo Pages
- Powerful Promotions
- Branding

There are so many great uses for a strong power pitch it's foolish to ignore it. The right short power pitch, used consistently, can create more awareness than shouting "Buy my book!" a million times on social media. And a great, really strong 25-30-word pitch can do more for creating awareness of your book than any number of different approaches combined. It's all about knowing how to write a great pitch, and being consistent when using that pitch.

There are three rules to writing a great pitch. Your pitch must convey:

1. The genre (without stating the genre)
2. The target audience (without stating the audience)
3. The story

This pitch must be between 25 and 30 words, it must be written as well as your book, and it must really grab the reader. Notice that the story is last on this three-rule list. Unfortunately, some writers create pitches that talk about nothing but the story and somehow, they never convey the genre or who would love the book. It's an easy trap, but if you always remember to put the story last as you create your 25-30-word pitch, it will always make an impact.

Here are some really great 25-30-word pitches. These examples take each rule into consideration and display strong, succinct writing.

What happens to a vampire after he finally dies? Heaven? Hell? Nope, purgatory in a West Hollywood warehouse. Go figure.

- This pitch is great because one can clearly see it's urban fantasy, the audience is most likely female, and the story has a tongue-in-cheek humor to it.

Retired Victorian spy, Constance Shaw, is intent on living a proper life. However, a missing sister, insistent queen, and a mysterious American force her hand and change her plans forever.

- This is great because the historical genre is clear, the pitch is written in a style that shows the writer's skill with that genre, the story looks unique, and I can see the target audience is women who read historical adventures.

Desperate to escape her tortured past, a teenage genius learns she has multiple personality disorder when she's arrested for the kidnap and murder of her four-year-old half-sister.

- This is great because this YA thriller pitch hits hard, conveys the genre, the target audience, and tells enough of the story to intrigue.

An anarchist punk faery with mob ties takes on one last job, with the help of a vengeful shape-shifting slave soldier in 1979 Philadelphia.
- This is great because one can see that it's an urban fantasy, it's a well written sentence, shows originality, and shows that fantasy lovers with a sense of humor are the primary target market.

In a starving, near-future America, a betrayed mercenary lives in quiet anonymity until a woman whose secret could feed the world demands his help…and reawakens his brutal past.

- This is great because I can see the apocalyptic horror element, understand the target audience, and this pitch shows just enough sizzle to make it very interesting.

Rafe Bennett is an old-west, hard-riding outlaw. Vivi is the Angel assigned to watch over him. When she falls from heaven and into his arms, Lucifer assures that all hell breaks loose.

- This one is great because I can see that it is a romance, recognize the angel unique hook within the story, and see the historic sub-genre. The audience and story originality are clear.

Now it's time for you to write your own Short Power Pitch. Don't worry if it's a little long, editing is our friend. Write as many versions as you need to find the perfect pitch. The final pitch should be between 25-30 words, and written as well as your book. Don't be intimidated, you can do this!

SPECIAL NOTE: If you are writing a series of books, it is always a great idea to write a singular 25-30-word pitch for that entire series as a branding tool, in addition to writing the short pitch for each individual book.

Remember the rules. Your pitch must convey:

1. The genre (without stating the genre)
2. The target audience (without stating the audience)
3. The story

My Short Power Pitches

Now go back and take a critical look at your short power pitch. Is it written well enough? Is it maybe too long or too short? Does it tell just the right amount of your story and not too much?

Here's a tip—read your pitch aloud. If it doesn't roll off your tongue smoothly, rework it. If the words make you stumble, rethink your word choices. If you can't memorize it and say it at a moment's notice, it might be too complex.

And finally, can you live with the pitch you've written? This pitch will never change for that book. It will appear exactly the same on every post, every press release, every query letter, every promotion, on your website, and blog. It will be the opening part of your back-cover blurb and a powerful beginning for your synopsis. It never changes because that pitch will become the BRANDING for that book. Changing it will water down, or even eliminate, the power of the pitch. Make sure it's great, says what you want it to say, follows the rules, and that you can vocalize it fluidly.

Think about this a bit. A business needs a branding pitch. Services of every kind use great power pitches. You can write a terrific short pitch for your favorite pizza, or movie, or song. Thinking in succinct clips, using the right words, can only improve your writing and your pitches. Pay attention to the marketing world around you. Everybody is pitching something all the time. Some pitches are so fantastic you can't forget them. We might think of them as slogans or tag lines but they're power pitches, through and through.

Now that you see the importance of mastering the creation of great short pitches, I'm going to show you how to give that pitch even more PUNCH!

SOUND BITES THAT BITE HARDER

I hear you. "What? Make the pitch even shorter!" I know, you think I'm nuts but there's an important reason for having a 10-word sound bite in your marketing arsenal.

Let's start at the top. What is a sound bite? It's the most basic comment about your book that you can make, with the most impact you can create. A sound bite can be (okay, now you're really going to hate me) AS FEW AS 10 WORDS AND AS MANY AS 15 WORDS.

To explain this a little better, I want you to imagine that you're standing in a receiving line with a hundred other authors. Those other authors have written books in different genres, in the same genre, and in sub-genres. They've written non-fiction, how-to books, and memoirs. Some of them are top ten best-selling authors, and some of them are first-time authors.

Now, moving along this receiving line in front of you and all the other authors, is a line of hundreds of reporters, book buyers, book club leaders, and promotional people who can get your book in front of lots of book buyers. They are walking slowly, reaching out, briefly shaking your hand and they need to KEEP MOVING. That means you have mere seconds to get your sound bite out of your mouth and into their heads. It has to hook there so that when they get past all the other authors, they remember what YOU said.

This is an important lesson. No matter how unique your style or novel is, you are up against thousands of other authors for the readers ...

- **Attention**
- **Discretionary dollar**
- **Loyalty**

Walk around any book store or browse Amazon's book pages. How many other books are listed or stacked on the shelves with yours? How many other authors write the same genre you do? Now imagine every one of those books on the shelves or all those lovely covers on the Amazon pages are shouting a 10-word sound bite at you. Which one are you going to hear and which one are you going to remember?

That is the point of this lesson. How do you stand out? How do you get attention? And how do you compete?

Here are a few samples based on some of the sample short pitches shown earlier:

25-Word Pitch – *What happens to a vampire after he finally dies? Heaven? Hell? Nope, purgatory in a West Hollywood warehouse. Go figure.*

10-15-Word Sound Bite – *Can a vampire get into heaven? He can, but only through a West Hollywood warehouse.*

25-Word Pitch – *Retired Victorian spy, Constance Shaw, is intent on living a proper life. However, a missing sister, insistent queen, and a mysterious American force her hand and change her plans forever.*

10-15-Word Sound Bite – *Living a proper English life isn't in the cards for retired Victorian spy, Constance Shaw.*

25-Word Pitch – *Desperate to escape her tortured past, a teenage genius learns she has multiple personality disorder when she is arrested for the kidnap and murder of her four-year-old half-sister.*

10-15-Word Sound Bite – *Teenage genius with multiple personality disorder arrested for murder of her baby sister.*

25-Word Pitch – *Rafe Bennett is an old-west, hard-riding outlaw. Vivi is the Angel assigned to watch over him. When she falls from heaven and into his arms, Lucifer assures that all hell breaks loose.*

10-15-Word Sound Bite – *An angel and an old-west outlaw struggle against Lucifer to hold on to true love.*

Here's a little tip to help you write your sound bite. Think about a really strong newspaper headline, one that tells just enough of the juicy facts to make you want to read the story. That's what we're going for when writing a 10-15-word sound bite.

There are two parts to this little sound bite assignment.

PART ONE. Take one of your favorite books by another author and write a 10-15-word sound bite for that book. The reason for this is that as a reader, you are truly getting only what you learned from their book. You haven't known this author intimately, he/she hasn't told you what they wished was in the book, or what they removed from the book, or even what they hope you'd understand about the book. All you know is the book. What you write as a sound bite for that book will come from what the book actually says.

PART TWO. This will be very simple. Take your 25-word pitch and make it shorter by half, no more than 10–15 words. These 10–15 words must tell your story with impact and power. I need to get a glimpse of the genre and I need to WANT to know more.

Other Author's Book Sound Bite Assignment Part 1

Take one of your favorite books by another author and write a 10-15-word sound bite for that book.

My Sound Bite
Assignment Part 2

Write your 10-15-word sound bite.

Were you able to do the same thing with your own sound bite as you did with the other author's sound bite? The trick is to step away from your book, from the emotions of it and the love for it, and simply punch hard with the most effective elements that tell the story. You can do it for books you read, and in order to really make your sound bite explosive, you must be able to step away and do it with your own book, too.

LOCATING YOUR QUERY TARGETS

What's a target? That all depends on what you're shooting for. Targets can be very different depending on the goal.

Imagine your book, *WIZARD CLAN,* is a fantasy about the very first wizard ever. Now imagine you want to do a book event for *WIZARD CLAN*. I don't need to think hard to know where your head immediate went. You started thinking of every book store you know, right? That's because most authors see their book as simply a book, and believe that book buyers only buy books in book buying environments. It's a terribly uncreative way to look at marketing your wonderful product. *WIZARD CLAN* deserves much more.

Now, putting on your creative marketing thinking cap, and let's try this again. Where would you like to do an author event, the kind of event where you speak to the attendees, do a reading from the book, then sell and sign copies of *WIZARD CLAN*? These are the places that come to mind for me:

- New Age shops where they sell crystals and tarot cards
- Magic and hobby shops
- A dinosaur park showing how life might have been when your wizard clan discovered magic and how to use it

- A museum featuring a shaman or aboriginal peoples exhibit
- A Renaissance Fair

So, why might I suggest such places for a book event? Other authors do their events in book stores and libraries, why should yours be different? Because different is good! Different is effective! Different works! And, different reaches bigger, more curious audiences.

If you hold your book event in a book store you are only reaching people thinking about buying a book at that moment, and most of them walked in searching for a particular book, not yours. You're also sitting there in a store loaded with a gazillion other books—all your competition for the money those people plan to spend. When you're Dan Brown, Diana Gabaldon, or Barbara Kingsolver you can do all the book events you want in book stores. People are coming to see YOU. Until you're famous, you need to get people's attention for your books, and you need to get that attention in many different, creative, and unique ways.

It's important to realize that your target audience for your book is far more than just the narrow, noisy places where most of your competition reaches out to them. Your book is different, loaded with unique elements that reach prospective book buyers in many places. The primary goal of a great marketing author is to identify as many audiences as possible for the unique elements inside your book, and reach them is as many places as possible. Those are your marketing targets for book sales.

There are other targets. The New Age shop is a target. How do you, an author of a cool book the shop's customers will love, connect with that shop owner? Literary agents are targets, small and large publishers are targets. Groups you'd like to reach out to, like book clubs and reader groups are targets. How do you reach out to these targets?

With a targeted query.

Obviously, you already know how to capture the right contacts within a particular target—the agents who represent your genre, the publishers seeking books like yours, the shops, parks, pet stores, golf shops, *whatever shops* that perfectly fit in with your story's unique hooks. Locating the right contact and gaining an understanding of the location helps you say the right things in your query letter. Making that query a win/win for both you and the recipient is the trick. Understanding that there are many, many places to query for book exposure is important. Be open. Be creative. Use that wonderful imagination. Look for targets where other authors never even think of going.

Marketing is creating awareness. Having a ton of targets helps you create broader awareness than you ever imagined.

SYNOPSIS, BLURBS, AND PITCH POWER

Where and how do you use these wonderful pitches? We covered a brief list earlier. You need branding pitches and sound bites for:

- Queries—and a query is for far more then querying a literary agent
- Book and Back Cover Blurbs
- Synopsis
- Press Releases
- Easy Tweet Posts
- Limited Posts for Promo Pages
- Powerful Promotions
- Branding

When querying a literary agent or publisher, it's best to use the 25-word pitch right up front. However, when querying a unique hook location for a book signing, it's far better to open your letter with an introduction and explanation of your idea. Explain how it's a win/win for both the location and you, then the pitch, showing how and why your book is loaded with things the location's customers/patrons already love.

Your 25-30-word power pitch is perfect as an open for your book blurb, and it starts a synopsis off with a bang.

When writing press releases, that pitch is the explanation of your book, and works best after stating the reason for your press release, for example an event or charity connection.

These pitches and sound bites are wonderful tools for social media activity. Tweet and Facebook away using your sound bite and short pitch to kick off the message or to be the message. Use the sound bite on your Instagram account whenever you post a pic related to your book's unique hooks. Use the sound bite on Pinterest posts that work with your book's unique elements.

Remember all those little bio's you need to have for your social networks? *Author of WIZARD CLAN* is nice, but imagine that with a really strong sound bite. Now your Twitter followers will see *Lover of magic. Author of WIZARD CLAN, where magic blasted from the earth's very beginnings.*

Now let's move a little further into the author life challenges, like all those Promo Groups, Websites, and Pages that require a very brief description of your book. BAM, done! When you're already armed with the perfect branding pitch, it's so much easier than reinventing a description every time you want to participate in a promotion or be listed.

And finally, your book's branding is in your hands. Every time you connect with anyone related to your author life, you need to use that branding pitch. It needs to be a primary focus of your email signature, a highly visible part of your book website, very clearly displayed on your blog. It should be on your business card, and on any promotional item you choose to create—bookmarks, post cards, etc.

This is where a great series branding pitch can work well. It will carry you through all the books within that series, yet still allow you space to promote each book pitch as it becomes available.

This is power. When you and your books become identified with that branding pitch, you've made an impact. When reviewers are repeating that branding pitch in their reviews, you've reached a point of connection. Using your words this way makes marketing simple, powerful and, best of all, effective. You will have created awareness that in turn, creates sales results.

Now, make a list of as many ways and places as you can think of for using your branding pitch and sound bite!

Using My Branding Pitch and Sound Bite

THE PERFECT QUERY FOR EVERY NEED

It would be absolutely fantastical if one query would work for everything, wouldn't it? Just fill in the name and done. Well, fantastical is the right word, because it isn't real. We've left the Shire and journeyed into the world of business where query writing is a make-it or break-it opportunity. The good news is that your creativity is in your suitcase and ready to come out the minute you need it. For now, we have to be professional and connect with our target for the results we're seeking.

The following are examples of:

- A query to a literary agent
- A query to a small or mid-size publisher
- A query to create a promotional event
- A press release (also a query)
- A query for a unique location book event

Note how these pitch elements are used within the letter, where they're used in the letter structure, and especially notice the special attention to how each query approaches the receiver. After each sample query, I would like you to write one for your book. I've chosen one of the sample 25-30-word pitches for these examples.

25-Word Pitch – *What happens to a vampire after he finally dies? Heaven? Hell? Nope, purgatory in a West Hollywood warehouse. Go figure.*

LITERARY AGENT QUERY LETTER EXAMPLE

Dear Ms. Brittany Banks,

I would like to thank you in advance for your time and consideration of my book. *Cold in California* is book one of a three book series, it is 90,000 words and complete. I am contacting you because of your expressed interest in unique and twisted urban fantasy with a touch of humor.

What happens to a vampire after he finally dies? Heaven? Hell? Nope, purgatory in a West Hollywood warehouse. Go figure.

Cold in California playfully proposes that even the worst of the supernatural world gets one more chance at redemption. Twice-baked vampire, Gabriel Strickland, learns this when he's whisked from his final demise and into a holding tank of sorts tucked secretly in West Hollywood. Sixty creatures, including other dead vampires, pixies, a legendary Navaho stick man and bothersome leprechauns, struggle together to earn brownie points (against their natures) and wait out possible centuries of purgatory. Gabriel receives dubious advice from Crudo Cushman, a controlling troll who runs the place, but there are always bugs in the pudding and he faces them all. Enter, the beautiful Dori Gallagher, who not only knocks Gabriel off his feet, but also an evil warlock who has designs on her.

His life after double death is all about balance, but when menacing forces gather against Gabriel and everything he's come to respect, it's a fiery clash of supernatural verses supernatural in one heroic effort to save his new reality.

As per your submissions guidelines, I have added the first 25 pages of the manuscript at the bottom of this email.

Again, thank you for your time. I look forward to hearing your thoughts.

Sincerely,
Mary Smith

Home address
Phone number
Website Link, Blog Link, Twitter Link, Facebook Link, LinkedIn Link

- **NOTE** the location of the 25-word pitch (underlined)

- **NOTE** the personalized introduction, clearly showing that the author has read the agent's bio and preferences.

- **NOTE** that the author does exactly what the submissions guidelines dictated, adding the first 25 pages at the end of the email and not as an attachment

- **NOTE** the information at the end of the letter. It is very important to list your links, because the first thing a literary agent does when they receive a query is Google you and check out your links for social media activity.

My Query Letter to a Literary Agent

PUBLISHER QUERY LETTER EXAMPLE

Dear Mr. Green,

I have always loved the books published by Green-Bellows Publishing. I especially love the unique paranormal and supernatural nature of the books you publish, and I would love to be a Green-Bellows author.

Thank you in advance for your time and consideration of my book. *Cold in California* is book one of a three book series, it is 90,000 words and complete.

<u>What happens to a vampire after he finally dies? Heaven? Hell? Nope, purgatory in a West Hollywood warehouse. Go figure.</u>

Cold in California playfully proposes that even the worst of the supernatural world gets one more chance at redemption. Twice-baked vampire, Gabriel Strickland, learns this when he's whisked from his final demise and into a holding tank of sorts tucked secretly in West Hollywood. Sixty creatures, including other dead vampires, pixies, a legendary Navaho stick man and bothersome leprechauns, struggle together to earn brownie points (against their natures) and wait out possible centuries of purgatory. Gabriel receives dubious advice from Crudo Cushman, a controlling troll who runs the place, but there are always bugs in the pudding and he faces them all. Enter, the beautiful Dori Gallagher, who not only knocks Gabriel off his feet, but also an evil warlock who has designs on her.

His life after double death is all about balance, but when menacing forces gather against Gabriel and everything he's come to respect, it's a fiery clash of supernatural verses supernatural in one heroic effort to save his new reality.

As per your submissions guidelines, I've attached the full manuscript. Again, thank you for your time. I look forward to hearing your thoughts.

Sincerely,
Mary Smith

Home address
Phone number
Website Link, Blog Link, Twitter Link, Facebook Link, LinkedIn Link

- **NOTE** the location of the 25-word pitch (underlined)

- **NOTE** the personalized introduction, clearly showing that the author is familiar with the publisher and the books they publish
- **NOTE** that the author does exactly what the submissions guidelines dictated
- **NOTE** the information at the end of the letter. It is very important to list your links, because the first thing a publisher does when they receive a query is Google you and check out your links for social media activity.

My Query Letter to a Publisher

PROMOTIONAL IDEA PROPOSAL QUERY LETTER

EXAMPLE

June 1, 2018

Ms. Bernadette Carrol
Director Promotions
Los Angeles Blood Bank
123 Sepulveda Blvd.
Los Angeles, CA 11111

Dear Ms. Carrol,

I am contacting you because I would like to help the Los Angeles Blood Bank's efforts this fall. I am the author of an urban fantasy book entitled _Cold in California_, and I'm proposing a FANG DONOR event in an effort to assist the Blood Bank in getting donors and donations.

What happens to a vampire after he finally dies? Heaven? Hell? Nope, purgatory in a West Hollywood warehouse. Go figure. _Cold in California_ playfully proposes that even the worst of the supernatural world gets one more chance at redemption.

I am organizing an online effort to bring blood and cash donations to the Los Angeles Blood Bank locations during the week of October 25th through 31st. Fans of vampire books, shows, and films will have the opportunity to log on to a website designed especially for this event and either commit to making a physical donation of blood, or a cash donation to the Los Angeles Blood Bank. Every fan who commits will receive a FANG DONOR NUMBER which they will present when they make a blood donation, or place on their check when they send in their cash donation.

The goal is to bring in hundreds of blood donors and thousands of dollars to the Blood Bank. I will be promoting this event on my social media, and recruiting other vampire book authors and their fans to participate and pass on the information through their social networks. I request that the Los Angeles Blood Bank also make the event known on social media. I will also be sending out press releases about the event for media coverage.

For the FANG DONORS, the vampire book writers and I will pull together three prizes—baskets of our books, red wine, glass wine glasses, chocolate covered cherries, sunglasses, and a tee shirt that says "FANG DONOR for the Los Angeles Blood Bank."

I look forward to hearing your thoughts on this and any ideas you might add to help us help with your autumn blood drive needs.

Sincerely,
Mary Smith

Home address
Phone number
Website Link, Blog Link, Twitter Link, Facebook Link, LinkedIn Link

- **NOTE** the date when this proposal was sent, easily a full four months before the event
- **NOTE** the location of the 25-word pitch (underlined)
- **NOTE** the clear explanation of the proposal and reasons for the event, to help the Blood Bank at a time that works well for the Blood Bank and the urban fantasy lovers (Halloween)
- **NOTE** that the author states her plans and commitments to the project
- **NOTE** the clear invitation for any ideas from the Blood Bank. Many discussions will follow and needs discussed, like the need for the Blood Bank's logo for the tee shirt and any flyers used
- **NOTE** the information at the end of the letter. It is very important to list your links. Showing off your links tells the reader that you are socially networked and can do what you proposed in the letter

My Promotional Idea Query Letter

PRESS RELEASE

For Immediate Release

Contact: Mary Smith
marysmith@marysmith.com
(123) 456-7890

FANG DONORS CONVERGE ON LOS ANGELES

Dateline, October 22, 2018. New York City: Mary Smith is the author of *Cold in California*, the vampire book that asks: <u>What happens to a vampire after he finally dies? Heaven? Hell? Nope, purgatory in a West Hollywood warehouse. Go figure.</u>

Ms. Smith has taken her playful blood obsession several steps further. She has pulled together authors of urban fantasy vampire books in the Los Angeles area to help the Los Angeles Blood Bank with a fun and very needed FANG DONOR event to be held from October 25 through Halloween night, October 31.

Go to www.FANGDONOR.ORG to register to make a blood or cash donation to help the Los Angeles Blood Bank during this critical period. Donations are always welcome, but need is especially high during the fall and winter months. When a donor registers, they will receive a FANG DONOR number that will identify them as part of this special charity event. Present the number when donating blood, or place the number on their check for donations made out to the Los Angeles Blood Bank.

Blood donations can be made at any Los Angeles Blood Bank location, the list to be found on the Los Angeles Blood Bank website, www.labloodbank.org . Cash donations can also be made through that Los Angeles Blood Bank website, using the FANG DONOR number assigned.

All participating FANG DONORS are eligible to win one of three grand prize gift baskets which include urban fantasy vampire books written by the twelve participating authors, two bottles of Colter Farms Red Wine, four wine glasses, two pounds of Swiss Sunshine Chocolate Covered Cherries, two pairs of The Eye Guys sunglasses, a tube of Natural Living Sun Screen and a tube of Natural Living Skin Conditioner, and two "FANG DONOR for the Los Angeles Blood Bank" tee shirts.

For more information please contact Mary Smith at marysmith@marysmith.com or (123) 456-7890. You can also contact the Los Angeles Blood Bank Director of Events, Ms. Roberta Carrol at rcarrol@labloodbank.com or (123) 876-5432.

- **NOTE** the date when this press release goes out. Never send out a press release too early, but always give enough time for the reporter to contact you for more information

- **NOTE** the location of the 25-word pitch (underlined) and how it explains the connection between the author and the event

- **NOTE** the clear explanation of the event, to help the Blood Bank at a time of need. This is NEWS

- **NOTE** that the press release is filled with facts and only facts

- **NOTE** the websites information. This is vital because many newspapers or radio stations will only state exactly what is in the press release, so it has to be complete

- **NOTE** the listing of the items in the gift baskets and the companies that donated those items. Everyone gets credit. The authors are not listed because they are listed, along with their book covers, on the back of the tee shirt as the FANG DONOR GANG

- **NOTE** the clear contact at the top and throughout the press release. This is so that the reporter can contact you for more information or to participate in any way. A good press release is a query for the press to respond and reach out to help

My Press Release

UNIQUE LOCATION BOOK EVENT QUERY LETTER

May 9, 2018

Dear Mr. Walker,

I have always loved your wonderful COSPLAY COSTUME SHOPPE. It's the kind of place that spurs the imagination and makes us all feel like kids again.

My name is Mary Smith and I am the author of *Cold in California*. <u>What happens to a vampire after he finally dies? Heaven? Hell? Nope, Purgatory in a West Hollywood warehouse. Go Figure.</u> *Cold in California* playfully proposes that even the worst of the supernatural world gets one more chance at redemption.

That playfulness is the reason I am contacting you. I would love to hold a book event in your fantastic store. The open area to the right of the store entrance is perfect for a table, my books and me. I will promote the event to all of my local friends and fans, provide flyers for your window and front desk, and even incorporate some of your wonderful costumes as part of my presentation. I will be sending out press releases to the local media, as well as posting flyers everywhere I can. I also plan to incorporate an interactive Facebook Event live during that evening, as well as use Twitter and Instagram to show pics, show off the costumes, and my book covers.

The event would take two hours, include a reading, a brief speaking engagement, and a book signing. The costumed characters will come from the back of the store on cue with the reading and speaking elements to bring attention to your great products for rent and purchase. I will be bringing red wine and chocolate covered cherries to serve to those attending.

For this event, I will only require a table and two chairs. I'll decorate the table and area as well as have some music playing to attract attention. My intentions are to bring you new customers, and that your attending customer base might bring book sales.

I would love to do this on a Saturday, sometime in July, from 6 – 8 p.m. I look forward to hearing your thoughts and ideas. Please feel free to call me at (123) 456-7890 to discuss this event and how we can make it great for us both.

Sincerely,
Mary Smith

Home address

Phone number
Website Link, Blog Link, Twitter Link, Facebook Link, LinkedIn Link

- **NOTE** the date when this proposal was sent, a few months before the suggested event

- **NOTE** the flattering open about the location, and how much the author likes it, as well as why it fits perfectly with the book she's promoting

- **NOTE** the location of the 25-word pitch (underlined)

- **NOTE** the clear explanation of the event the author has in mind

- **NOTE** that the author makes SURE this is a win/win for both her and the store owner (Without a win/win, there's little chance of getting cooperation or raising interest)

- **NOTE** the clear invitation for any ideas from the store owner. This is where they get excited to participate and show off their merchandise

- **NOTE** the invitation to call her to discuss the idea further

- **NOTE** the information at the end of the letter. It tells the shop owner that the author is an active and promotionally minded person

My Unique Location Book Event Query Letter

LESSON TWO
HOOKING BOOK BUYERS

The most terrifying part of having a book to market is the part where you need to locate and identify your book buyer so that you can talk to them. That's the moment when all your confidence about how wonderful and well-loved your book will be starts to shatter and your knees start to shake. How do you locate the buyers for your specific book? Where are they? What do you say to them? You already know that shouting "Buy my book!" isn't a great strategy, that's why you're here. But if you don't shout "Buy my book!" what on earth are you supposed to do?

This is a painfully normal reaction to marketing. Even I, a person with decades of marketing experience under my belt, faced that same terror when my first fiction was released. It didn't seem like a product, which I clearly knew how to market and create great sales for. It was my book, my baby, the thing I stayed up nights worrying about and spent my days perfecting.

Guess what? It is a product. As uncomfortable as it may feel at first to face that fact, it's important to do so quickly. It's really hard to sell your baby because you will always want to explain it, clean it up, make excuses for it, pamper it, defend and protect it. But a product is a solid entity standing on its own. Once you think of your book as a product, knowing how to reach out, locate, and hook your book buyers becomes exciting, creative, and a lot of fun.

I promise you, what follows is not what you expect. Open your mind and let the ideas start to flow as you explore these techniques. Other authors don't think this way so already you're setting you and your book apart. Be brave and have a blast. Be sure to strap in, this roller coaster ride leads to some amazing heights.

LOCATING UNIQUE HOOKS

Contrary to what most of your author friends think, this process does NOT start with Facebook book promotional groups or on Twitter with cover reveals. It starts someplace completely different. Great marketing starts INSIDE YOUR BOOK. It starts with your STORY. Finding the perfect book buyer is all about what you wrote and who loves those things. It's all about looking at marketing from the inside of your story out, instead of the other way around.

Locating and using your unique hooks as the basis for searching out audience gives you a broader, larger, and multi-level approach to marketing. But before you do anything, you need to dig in and locate those unique hooks.

Before we begin, know that there are two different kinds of unique hooks. There are unique STORY hooks that set your story apart from others in the genre—like, for example, yellow dragons. And there are unique MARKETING hooks that lead to an audience—like magic, that lead to wizards, and magic shows, and films, and television programs on related subjects. Few people specifically love yellow dragons, but a whole lot of people can be found in a whole lot of places that love the concept of magic.

This searching technique works for fiction of any genre and it works for nonfiction, too. It's all about locating the powerful hooks inside your book that connect with people. Here are a few examples:

- **A Nonfiction** about organizing one's closets = an audience of professional people, busy mothers, business people, charity organizations, and more
- **A Women's Fiction** about a woman traveling the world after the loss of her husband = an audience of people who love to travel, people who love cultures, people who belong to support groups, and women in general (which is a massive audience)
- **A Mystery** that focuses on an avid gardener discovering a dead body under his petunias and solving the murder = an audience of people who love gardening, people who love television shows and films about solving murders, and love true crime
- **An Historic Romance** focused on the Civil War period = an audience of lovers of the period, of vintage clothing and antiques from that period, of Civil War reenactors, of films and television programs about or set in the Civil War Era, and of course, since this is romance, women everywhere
- **A High Fantasy** that tells the story of how the Fae have slipped into the wrong reality and must get back to their own world and time safely = an

audience of fantasy lovers, Cos Play lovers, fantasy film and television lovers, and fantasy gamers

- **An Historic Nonfiction** that explores weapons and battle strategies throughout history = an audiences of antique lovers, antique weapons collectors, people fascinated with war and battle throughout history, and people who love television and film documentaries about various battles and wars

These examples are just the tip of the iceberg. They only touch on one specific unique hook but there are many unique marketing hooks inside your book. All of those hooks lead to an audience. Some of those audiences are massive, some are smaller, but all are additional audiences in places where no other author has even thought to go.

I'm sure you noticed that genre is not a unique hook, and there's a reason for that. Because so many authors, all your competition, start and end their marketing focus on genre and nothing but genre, those audiences are already inundated with "Buy my book!" shouts. Effective marketing strategically reaches out to a targeted market and builds market upon market for larger exposure. The reason unique hooks help you and your book stand apart from the crowd is simply because the crowd (your competition) is someplace else, crawling over each other, hoping to get a sale.

The first issue for most authors when starting this process, is that they can't recall all their unique hooks. Trust me, you've written all the audiences you need right into your story. You're already a marketing genius and didn't even know it! All you have to do is dig.

Here's a question for you. When was the last time you actually read your book? Most authors never open the book once it's published, some never look at it after the final edit. Over time, all you remember is the cover, the pitch, the blurb and that you have to market it to gain sales. Your baby has become a stranger and it's time to get reacquainted.

I strongly suggest that you open that book and read it from cover to cover. Keep a notebook handy and jot down all the unique hooks that lead to audience. Remember the difference between a unique marketing hook and a unique story hook. If you write down a wonderful hook but can't visualize the audience, it isn't a marketing hook. Avoid listing things like *challenging*, or *bravery*, or, well, *yellow dragons*. These words might describe your story, but they do not lead to an audience. Our goal here is to locate as many unique marketing hooks that lead to audience possible.

Take your time and read your book, then list as many unique MARKETING hooks as you can find in there. WARNING: a cat is not a unique hook if she only shows up on page 38 and never again. A unique hook is prevalent throughout the story, has direct effect on the protagonist and antagonist, and drives the story. If the story would be drastically different without a particular unique hook, it's definitely an appropriate unique hook for this technique. Also, if some of your hooks are too similar, they're not additional hooks. Each unique hook should appear on your list only once. (A train, and a train engine, and a train caboose are not three unique hooks. Choose just one.)

My Unique Marketing Hooks

IDENTIFYING _YOUR_ AUDIENCE

Now that you've located the marketing hooks inside your book, let's talk about how to clearly define where YOUR audience is and how to reach out to them.

YOUR audience is no other author's audience. In the broader strokes, yes, perhaps you wrote a horror and many other horror authors are out there trying to sell their books. However, YOUR audience is different because there are unique things in your story that make it different and easier to market. This is more than just approaching horror genre book buyers and book clubs. YOUR audience is connected to the unique hook elements you wrote into your story. They are ready and waiting, seldom approached by authors, never shouted "Buy my book!" at, and very receptive because you will have found a way to reach out and connect to them in places other authors have not thought of.

The key to identifying your audience, where to reach them, and how to talk to them takes a tiny shift in thinking. Remember, people who buy books are not always walking around book stores, trolling Facebook Book Sales groups, seeking a good book on Twitter, or slithering around Amazon in search of their next read. People are out in the world, going to the grocery store, the dry cleaners, the gardening shops, the hobby shops, pet shops, shoe stores, tattoo shops, whatever floats their boat. And they are socializing on Facebook, Twitter, Instagram, and Pinterest about the things they love. They're just living their lives and that does not revolve around buying books.

You have written a book that just happens to have things in the story that a lot of people love. Reaching out to them where other authors do, shouting on Facebook and Twitter, is like shouting (along with thousands of your competition) into the same megaphone, at the same time, at just a small sliver of the actual book-buying population. It's foolish and a waste of time.

Now, let's imagine that you, unlike all your author friends, decide to do this whole marketing thing differently. Sure, you can post on FB and Twitter to all the book sales groups but in addition to that, you work with your book's unique hooks for broader and larger audience exposure.

Let's imagine your book (no matter the genre) revolves around the patrons and staff of a tattoo shop (or a manicure shop, or gardening center, or any number of things.) The first question to ask yourself is where are people who love tattoos hanging out together?

Begin with your standard online venues. Facebook, for example. Simply type the word tattoo in the search box and then search GROUPS. You will see a list of hundreds of tattoo groups there. Some of these groups are huge with as many as 40,000 members, some groups are smaller, in the hundreds. If you take the time to look through the groups, you will find that many of them are perfect for you and your message, they show and discuss tattoos, the culture, the cost, the trials and tribulations of getting, changing, and removing tattoos. Make a list of twenty of these groups then study them carefully, check out the rules, and choose ten groups to join.

You can only join these groups from your personal Facebook account, not an author or business page, so be sure to write your bio for personal account carefully, telling people you like tattoos and have written a book about a tattoo shop.

Now, before we go further, remember. You are not joining these groups to socialize. You're not joining them to get tattoos. You're not joining them to get into daily discussions with new friends. And you are definitely NOT joining them to shout "Buy my book!"

You are joining them to CONNECT. Connection means value-added posts like offering pics of great tattoos (with a link to your book website,) posting articles and blog entries about tattoos (which can be found with a simple "tattoos" Google alert,) writing your own blog entries about tattoo history, improvements, health issues, etc. You would post something on these groups at least once a week on a Tuesday, Wednesday, or Thursday, which are the most focused days of the week. You could create a blog dedicated to tattoos and use that as an additional platform, bringing tattoo lovers to the blog. Once a month (and no more than once a month) you would post something about your book, the book buy link, a tiny excerpt, something you know will interest the members of those tattoo unique hook Facebook groups.

Every group has rules, so be sure to respect them. Never push your book too much. First you must connect, talk about what *they* are interested in, occasionally when you are on the group page, skim down and "like" or comment on something there. Connection means they like, and trust, and accept you into their group. However, never forget you are not there to socialize, so be careful to avoid that time-sucking trap. You are there to connect with the group's members because they happen to love the unique hook in your book.

Your book is about tattoos and this is YOUR audience. You'll find no other authors there, just people loving and sharing things about tattoos, which they love. Every few months add a few more Tattoo groups until you have thirty or forty appropriate groups. Never post to more than ten groups at a time, this will keep the Facebook police at bay.

Do a search of one of your book's unique hooks and list twenty Facebook groups, then choose ten groups to start with that will fit your marketing needs perfectly.

My Unique Hook Facebook Groups

Now, let's take a look a Twitter. The primary goal of Twitter is to load your account with people who love the unique hooks in your book(s) and NOT OTHER AUTHORS! It's sad, but authors tend to have hundreds or even thousands of other authors in their Twitter account. Other authors are your competition, and although other authors do buy books, they will never get you to the best seller list, so stop following other authors. Purge them out of your Twitter account. Join them on hash-tag events to keep in touch, but always remember, Twitter and Facebook are MARKETING TOOLS FOR BOOK SALES, not places to chat with other authors. Join author Yahoo groups, and a Facebook author group or two to keep in touch with them, share craft tips and just commiserate. But when you market, focus on just your target audiences. You'll be amazed how much and how fast this little effort can create results

Now, how do you find tattoo lovers on Twitter? There are no Twitter groups, so you need to be a little crafty. Think about television shows about tattoos, and there are lots of them. In the Twitter search box, look up the television show *Ink Master* Twitter account and take a look around. This account has tons of interesting posts and 282K followers. Click on the followers button and see what's there—282K people who love tattoos! This is a gold mine.

Now you do not need to follow the *Ink Master* account, although it doesn't hurt. It may lead you to some blog links and stories you can re-tweet to your tattoo-loving audience. The real power of this *Ink Master* Twitter account is the followers. All you need do is follow, follow, follow. These people already love tattoos, will learn from your bio that you too love tattoos, so much so that you wrote a book about a tattoo shop. Twitter permits you to follow a lot of people every day. At the end of two weeks, take a look at your own followers/following list. Many of those people will have returned the follow. You can purge out those who have not followed you back then continue the search and follow process. It's easy, takes little time and thought, and will load your Twitter account with followers who love your unique hook.

You're on your way to building a great Twitter account targeted to one of your book's unique hooks. Don't limit yourself to one tattoo Twitter account. There are more television programs about tattoos with Twitter accounts, check them all out and follow their followers, too. Famous tattoo shops have Twitter accounts. Follow those followers as well.

Once you've built at least 600 to 1,000 followers who love tattoos, you can start connecting with them. Do yourself a favor and take a few minutes every day to add unique hook Twitter following. The bigger the following, the more chance you have of reaching those tattoo lovers as they slip through the constant feed.

It's time to get on Twitter, locate television programs, films, businesses, or organizations that have twitter accounts that lead to lovers of your unique hooks and make a list of them. Consider the size of their following, and take a look at their activity which will show you how relevant they are to the topic. List at least eight big Twitter accounts connected to your unique hook and prepare to follow, follow, follow!

My Twitter Unique Hook Resources

Now, what do you say to all your new Twitter followers? Tweet value-added information. Only push your book once or twice a week. Post ten tweets in the morning (one minute apart) and ten tweets in the afternoon (one minute apart) Monday through Friday. Vary your times each day. I usually write my tweets over the weekend, keeping them cool and fun, clever but not cryptic, and use hash-tags within the actual tweet to save character count. Never say too much, and never say too little. For example:

> *#Tattoo.heaven on earth. This you've got to see!*
> *www.MyBlog/tattooheaven.com*

> *#Ink makes the world go 'round! And #Tattoo ink makes it gorgeous as it spins! www.amazon.yourbookbuylink.com (AND A PIC OF YOUR BOOK COVER)*

> *#Tattoo #culture crunch hits West Los Angeles.*
> *www.articlefoundonhuffingtonpost.com*

Tweets like these say just enough to catch attention, and most importantly, have your Amazon sales link, or an article found in your Google Alerts, or lead the viewer to your blog entry. That blog entry has the link to your book buy link. It's a chain designed to create sales. You can tweet pics of tattoos, or tattoo equipment, or repaired and removed tattoos. You can CONNECT!

When you write your ten or twenty tweets for the week, make sure each tweet has a link leading to things you want the viewer to follow. Links to stories and articles about tattoos, links to your website, links to reviews, to your blog, to your Pinterest account loaded with tattoo art, to the actual book on Amazon, etc. Talk tattoos. That's what your followers are interested in.

There are other social networks, too. Instagram is hash-tag driven, discover how to use your Instagram hash-tags for huge tattoo lover following. There's Pinterest. There's live locations, like tattoo shops, where you can do book signings. There are great ideas that can work live and online, like tattoo contests, and tattoo artist interviews that you can post on your blog then blast all over your social networks.

These are not difficult directions to take your messaging on social media, they just require seeing this marketing thing differently and with creative enthusiasm.

AUDIENCE EXPANSION WITH ©*SuperGenre* TECHNIQUES

We've talked very little about genre because the topic has a habit of cornering an author into a very limited approach to marketing. When an author tells me they write romance, they automatically assume that the only places to reach romance readers is through romance Facebook book sales groups and Romance Book Clubs. As I mentioned earlier, those are fine to approach, but you need to realize that a million other romance authors are also shouting at the members there.

Let's take this a tiny bit further. Go to any Facebook Romance (or any other genre) Book Group and click on the group's members. Check out how many of them are OTHER ROMANCE AUTHORS. On average, every time you post on one of those genre specific book sales Facebook groups, only about 25% of the members are actual book buyers. The other 75% are your competition. Also remember, those authors are going on to that Facebook Group a lot more often than buyers, posting their "Buy my book!" posts relentlessly, hoping to get attention.

Now, let's go back to that romance book. The first, and most important, question I ask that romance author is, "What else is in your book?" Athletes? Musicians? Dancers? Loggers? Bakers? Financial advisers? Dogs? Cats?

Vampires? Then I ask, "Where does the story take place?" In a city? On an island? In a coffee shop? At a carnival? In a light house? A Victorian house? A cabin in the mountains. England? Africa? Amsterdam? And finally, I ask, "Who are the people that love those things and where can you find them?"

These are the real marketing questions an author needs to focus on because these are the effective marketing unique hooks. Suddenly that romance has a much larger, more diverse, and interesting marketing strategy because the real target audiences are vibrant and active.

I created the ©SuperGenre technique to help authors not only define their unique hooks, but extrapolate those hooks as far as possible for bigger, broader, and diverse target audiences in multiple places. In other words, this little three step technique can help you reach far more lovers of your unique hooks in more places and more ways than you might have imagined. This technique helps you create extended lists for several targeted audiences, all based on your book's unique hooks. It's one of those crazy rides down the waterslide that help you fly past the marketing barriers authors tend to create for themselves. Think of ©SuperGenre Techniques as your personalized roadmap to marketing success.

Here's how ©SuperGenre Techniques work.

In the *My Unique Marketing Hooks* assignment above, you came up with as many unique hooks as you can find in your story. Once you have a nice list of seven or eight *different* unique hooks, choose three of those hooks to work with.

STEP 1 – For this example I'm using a Women's Fiction. These are the three unique hooks I chose to work with.

- **Horses** (*because the main character breeds and raises horses*)
- **Inspirational Amputee** (*because she has overcome the loss of her leg*)
- **Green** (*because she lives a green life in Oklahoma*)

STEP 2 – Now, to further develop a ©SuperGenre for this book we need to take our thinking far beyond the traditional cubby-hole genre concept. The goal is to locate as many different or expanded audiences as possible under each of the primary unique hooks listed. Now these three unique hooks look like this:

- **Horses**/ Riding Boots/ Country Music/ Cowboy Hats/ Riding Stables/ Ranchers/ Cowboy Culture
- **Inspirational Amputee**/ Physical Rehabilitation/ Prosthetic Support Groups/ Disability Help Groups
- **Green**/ Ecological/ Sustainable/ Healthy/ All Natural

STEP 3 – And the final activity in this technique is to extrapolate as far as possible, all the places where one might locate people who love these unique hook extensions. By the time this process is over, you will have uncovered at least ten different ways to reach each of the primary ©SuperGenres. That's going to make your marketing job a whole lot easier, and all with the simple technique of stretching your mind a little. Check this out!

- **Horses/ *Riding Boots*,** cowboy boot shops and online stores, Twitter, Facebook groups, Instagram, Pinterest/ *Country Music*, Country Music Artists followers, country music fashion, local country music shows or jamborees, local country music radio stations, Twitter, Facebook groups, Instagram, Pinterest/ *Cowboy Hats*, cowboy hats and clothing brick and mortar and online stores, Twitter, Facebook groups, Instagram, Pinterest/ *Riding Stables*, riding gear and saddle shops, local riding shows or rodeos, Twitter, Facebook groups, Instagram, Pinterest/*Ranchers*, living off the land, cattle ranches, *Pioneer Woman* cooking show fans, Twitter, Facebook groups, Instagram, Pinterest/ *Cowboy Culture*, western movies and televisions shows, old west traveling art exhibits, post-Civil War history buffs (Jessie James, old west outlaws and law men), Twitter, Facebook groups, Instagram, Pinterest

- **Inspirational Amputee/ *Physical Rehabilitation*,** documentaries, films and television shows about active amputees, local programs that help with rehabilitation, Twitter, Facebook groups, Instagram, Pinterest/ *Prosthetic Support Groups*, charities that help attain prosthetics for those who cannot afford them, organizations that develop better prosthetics, Twitter, Facebook groups, Instagram, Pinterest/ *Disability*

Help Groups, groups that organize handicapped sports events, organizations that help the handicapped get around, charities that bring entertainment to the handicapped or take them to entertainment, Twitter, Facebook groups, Instagram, Pinterest

- **Green/ *Ecological***, recycling organizations and businesses, local groups that protect the environment, groups that educate people on recycling, Twitter, Facebook groups, Instagram, Pinterest/ ***Sustainable***, groups and organizations that help people garden, compost, replace what they take from the earth, and purchase carefully, avoiding fish and wildlife that are endangered, Twitter, Facebook groups, Instagram, Pinterest/ *Healthy*, foodies, eating well groups and organizations, clubs that teach the balance between food and activity, Twitter, Facebook groups, Instagram, Pinterest/ ***All Natural***, groups and organizations, stores and shops that feature all natural, free range, grain fed, pesticide free food and products like soap, cleaning products, etc. Twitter, Facebook groups, Instagram, Pinterest

As you can see, what began as three simple unique hooks, **Horses**, **Inspirational Amputee**, and **Green**, has become a massive list of targets and locations. Obviously, some of these directions lend themselves perfectly to social media. Locating country music artists on Twitter will be easy, and in that Twitter account following are the future followers of the author of this book. On Facebook, it also can be very easy to locate lovers of cowboy culture, country music fashion and lovers of all things CMA. Facebook and Twitter can also work very well to locate lovers of the Green category.

Under the Inspirational unique hook, it's pretty obvious that publicity—using the media to assist or participate in a charity event or effort—will work very well. Marketing is not publicity, but connecting your marketing efforts with a charity can bring a lot of book sales.

And in all situations, these targets can be reached through the creation of live book events or participation in live appropriate and related events.

NOTE: DO NOT PARTICIPATE IN LIVE BOOK EVENTS. Instead of putting yourself in a room full of other authors and their books, I'd rather see you in a Cowboy Hat Store doing a reading and book signing. It's unexpected, creative, and draws far more attention to your book and no one else's.

It's time to build your own ©SuperGenre! You've read through your book and located your story' unique marketing hooks, so take these three simple steps.

> Step 1 – Choose three strong unique marketing hooks
>
> Step 2 – Expand those unique hooks to as many different audiences as you can
>
> Step 3 – Extrapolate those audiences for as many different locations as possible

Here you go!

My ©SuperGenre

BEING GENUINE AND MAKING CONNECTIONS

This is just a reminder of things we may have all forgotten since kindergarten. Growing up and growing older makes is all a little rough around the edges. It makes us want to shut away in a quiet place where we can complain about the world. Unfortunately, marketing the wonderful book you've written requires something very different. Old or young, energetic or a little worse for the wear, we need to reach out and market in a way that attracts attention and gets our book noticed. Always remember, social networking is first and foremost, a tool for book sales.

That means connecting with people we don't know, and doing it in a way that creates interest. Here are six tips to help with this.

6 TIPS FOR GREAT INTERNET INTERACTION

1. Say what your audience wants to hear, not what you want to tell them. They are in a unique hook group because they love that hook, in this case, vintage cars. It isn't productive to post a blog link about how writing has changed your life. However, if you've written a series of blog entries about vintage

cars, and your book has a vintage car unique marketing hook, you have the audience to respond favorably!

2. Stay away from politics. No matter how passionate you are about it, never talk politics or engage in a political discussion while marketing your book. Especially avoid the topic in places where you market your book, and even if you have an itch to respond to someone's post, step away from the keyboard. There are other ways and places to voice your political views, it's just not in places where you hope to make book sales.

3. Never react to criticism. If someone is rude in response to a unique hook post you've made, let it slide, or notify the moderator. You are your book, and getting into a word volley with someone who climbed out of the wrong side of the bed makes your book look bad.

4. CONNECT! Talk about things that most interest the people you're talking with. Go the extra mile and have a Google Alert for all the unique hooks lovers you're connecting with on Facebook and Twitter. Never tweet that you just cleaned your toilet, or Instagram what you're having for lunch, UNLESS your book is about toilet cleaning products or cooking. Connect on topics your unique hook lovers care about.

5. Be genuine. If you see a post on one of your unique hook Facebook Groups, or on Twitter, or Instagram, that touches you, say so. If you see that someone has lost their mother, a few words of sympathy go a long way. If one of your vintage car unique hook followers posts a photo on Instagram of

a super 1968 refurbished GTO convertible that's really sharp, say so. On the other hand, don't do this all the time or without truth behind your comments. Remember that people can hear a smile over the phone, and they and sense insincerity on the internet, too.

6. If someone makes a comment on any of your posts on your unique hook Facebook groups, be sure to go over there and at least "like" the comment to confirm that you've seen it. If someone retweets your tweet, thank them. If someone makes a comment on your unique marketing hook blog entry, reply. The cyberworld can be so cold, it takes very little to warm it up, and at the same time, warm prospective book buyers up to you, too.

LESSON THREE
GROWING AUDIENCE

Sometimes an author has a successful book launch, selling the number of books they felt respectable, then they sit tight and smile, feeling the glow of success. It was a success and they should feel good, but whatever that sales number was, we always want more. I once had a client who used the unique hook techniques I teach and sold seven thousand books in her first three weeks after book launch. It was wonderful. However, when her second book was written and released, she sold only a few hundred and called, wondering when went wrong. Simple. She dropped the ball, big time.

The thing to remember is that you never have enough audience. You can't disappear for a year and imagine book buyers will buy your next book like they bought the first one. The difference is marketing. For her second book, that author did not market. She assumed her fans were loyal, but fans are fickle. They follow the Pied Piper whistling loudest and forget about the one that sat back to enjoy their past success. Loyal fans only remain loyal fans if you continue to connect with them, and sales only grow if you continue to build audience. It's simple math.

Let's imagine you belong to five Facebook Groups, all focused on your unique hook, Country Music. The membership of those groups might look like this:

- Country Music Lovers – 115,000 members
- Guitar Country Love - 88,000 members
- CMA Fans of America – 200,000 members
- Fans of Joe Smith, Country Music Artist – 40,000 members
- Dixie Chicks Fans! – 75,000 members

This adds up to a total of 518,000 members that may see your post. The reality is that within these groups, there is usually a top 20% that are extremely active, so that means that your posts are actually connecting to and being seen by about 100,000 people. That's good, but all 100,000 people cannot be expected to buy a book.

However, it's far worse with those book sales Facebook Groups all the authors use. Some of them have as many as 80,000 members, but first you need to delete the number of authors in those groups, which is usually as many as 75%. So, an 80,000 membership is actually 20,000 book buyers. Of those book buyers how many are looking at the Facebook Group that day? How many love your genre? How many will click onto your buy link?

Now look at Twitter. Consider that only 1% of your Twitter following is actually looking at their Twitter feed the moment you post your tweet. A wonderful Twitter account loaded with 6,000 unique hook followers actually reaches 60 people. This is why I suggest tweeting ten different tweets, one each minute, twice a day, and shifting your times each day. It enhances the reach ratio.

This works the same with all of your networks, a small percentage of the people you're talking to are actually there, listening, interested in connecting, and finally willing to buy your book. It might feel a bit futile, but never fear. There are solutions for this.

Want more sales? For your back list? For the next book in a series, or a new book with the same unique hooks? Of course, you do. There are several ways to do that, and none of them allow time off for sitting on one's laurels, or whining about the system. It's time to learn how to use the system to your advantage, and this is all about numbers.

Take a look at all the Facebook groups you belong to, do the math, eliminating the 75% of other authors, focusing on the 20% most active unique hook group membership, adding your Twitter and Instagram 1%. Do the math. How many people are you actually reaching when you market?

My Numbers

How Many People I WANT to be Reaching

_____

_____

_____

Growing audience does include better attention to the numbers on Twitter and Facebook groups, but it also requires attention to other marketing venues in your life, the kind most authors ignore. It requires looking more places and using more venues most authors never think about. Let's go on a journey to grow your audience!

PLATFORMS THAT WORK HARD

What are your Platforms? Let's start at the top.

Your platforms are very important. Some authors like to use social media as their only platforms but it's just half the game. Your platforms are your WEBSITE, your BLOG, and your REAL-LIFE VISIBILITY. All three platforms are extremely important and you shouldn't shrug any of them off. Platforms are the planks that you build everything upon. They are sturdy, vibrant and alive, serve as powerful venues for information, and show your professionalism.

Most everything I teach does not cost money, but if you don't have a website and are not able or interested in building a website yourself, you may want to hire a web designer. However, remember, a website isn't a stagnant yet pretty bronze statue. It's a living, breathing, changing thing, and requires that you either pay your web master to do regular monthly updates, or learn how to make those updates yourself.

YOUR WEBSITE—Your website can be glitzy or simple, but it must have a few very important elements.

- **An Introduction Page**
    - This page talks about your books, what makes them unique, and why you write them. It's a great page to splash quotes from a few

great reviews. This page should be visually attractive and inviting, follow the theme and genre of your books, and have a navigation bar for all the other pages.

- **An Author Page**
  - This page is the professional you, has a photo of you, and gives a professional bio along with a few added personal bits of information—*Maryanne writes in a she shed hidden in her garden, accompanied by her English bulldog Sophie, and bird song floating into the window*. Maybe add a pic of that she shed and Sophie.

- **Book(s) Pages**
  - My suggestion is to have a page for each book or series. This gives each book or series a world all its own on a background that ads to the experience. The book cover and all the buy links for every distributor belong on these pages.
  - IF YOU WRITE IN SEVERAL DIFFERENT GENRES, be careful to keep those genres separate. For example, you might have a link to the Fantasy Book pages, and a different link to the Mystery Book pages. If you write subgenres—romance, historical romance, paranormal romance—they are usually fine within the same book(s) pages. However, there is a ***WARNING***. If you write erotica and YA or children's books, they should

NOT be on the same website at all. The goal of your website is to focus on the customer. The grandmother purchasing a YA book for her granddaughter will not appreciate it shown alongside an erotica book. Always focus on the customer.
- The Books Page is like your store's showroom. It is meant to dazzle and excite people into clicking on those buy links.

- **Activities Page**
  - If your Books Page is your showroom, then your Activities Page and Media Room are your business offices. On your activities page, you are telling the viewer what you're up to and what you've accomplished. Go over to Amazon, copy the best reviews and past them on this page. List all your book release dates, list all your charity involvements (especially if they relate to your unique hook,) and list all your book signing events or speaking events. You will also list all your social networks on this page. This page should be updated monthly.

- **Media Room**
  - The media room is a place just for the media. Should a reporter want to do a story on you, they can go to this page and take whatever they need. The media room includes:
    - Downloadable author photo
    - Downloadable author bio

- Downloadable covers for each book
- Downloadable one-page for each book that includes the buy links, the distribution locations, the back-cover blurb, the cover art, and a few great review excerpts
- Downloadable press releases (press releases you've sent out listed by date of release)
- All of your links
- A contact link providing either your email address or a contact form. Check on these often because you will need to reply to the media quickly if they reach out.

The point of each website page is to get the most bang for your moment with the viewer. A good website informs, entertains, makes the media feel welcome, and tells everyone what you're up to. If you don't have anything in your activities page, it's time to start creating book events or participating in events related to your book's unique hooks.

Changes for My Website

YOUR BLOG—There are powerful marketing blog efforts, and there are time-wasting blog efforts. A perfect example of a time-wasting blog is one written about writing, editing, the author's trials and tribulations, and crazy complaints about the publishing industry. A marketing blog should not be filled with random ideas and topics. That's a writer's journal and fine, it's just not marketing. Excerpt blog entries, complaining blog entries, the "oh the difficulties of being a writer" blog entries, entries about one's family, entries about someone else's books. I've seen them all. They are not useful for anything but commiserating. That's not marketing and it's not getting you anywhere closer to the best seller list. It's time to realize that every effort we make to gain book sales must be focused on *actual* marketing. The best use of a blog is to create awareness for your book, its unique hooks that people love, and to connect with those people.

The most effective marketing blog effort is one that makes you the expert or go-to person for a specific unique hook. For example, if your book is a mystery and something supernatural, angels, are helping the detective solve the case, you have two unique hooks right there to connect with people. What can you blog about that would bring lovers of those unique hooks closer to you and your book?

You can blog about angels, angels card readers, angels throughout time, angels in movies and television, and human angels helping people. You can blog about stories you find (through Google Alerts) where people swear that an angel helped them survive, or get home for the Holidays, or avoid an awful accident. You can even ask your blog readers to let you know their experiences with angels, interview that reader, and focus a blog entry on their story.

Other things you can blog about are real detective stories, actually interview detectives in your local police department or local private investigators and see how they approach a crime, what kind of crimes are most interesting to them, and what stumps them while they do their work.

Now remember, you have already collected thousands of angel unique-hook lovers into your Twitter account and belong to all the angel Facebook Groups. You already have true crime lovers in your Twitter following and are part of true crime lovers Facebook groups, so you've got the places to promote each blog entry to gain exposure.

Things you must remember about blogging are:

- Blog every OTHER week, and make your blog entries go live on Tuesday, Wednesday, or Thursday
- ALWAYS end your blog entries with an open-ended question to invite your readers to comment
- NEVER FORGET to add a brief 25-word description of your book, the book cover, and the buy links at the end of every entry
- PROMOTE your blog entries on your social networks
- TAG your blogs appropriately—your name, your book title, angels, crime, detectives, books, etc

- MOST IMPORTANTLY, NEVER, *EVER* LET ANOTHER AUTHOR GUEST BLOG ON YOUR BLOG! This is very important. You've worked hard for your following and your fan base. Keep the competition at arm's length and focus on connecting with YOUR audience, specific to YOUR book, and developed for YOUR success. At the same token, don't bother guest blogging for other authors. They only want you to guest blog because they don't feel like blogging that week. Also, their followers aren't interested in you, they're interested in the blog owner. Besides, most of that author's blog followers are other authors anyway. Spend your time on more productive, targeted marketing

- IF YOU WANT TO GUEST BLOG, think about creating a blog tour just for your unique hooks. Search out blogs that focus on angels or true crime. If the blog has at least 500 followers, posts regularly, and gets comments from their readers, contact the blog owner. Offer to guest blog about your unique book because you feel that their following will enjoy the topic. Those bloggers are usually thrilled to have a real author guest blog. It's a great approach because none of your competition is there, and those blog followers are excited about you and your book. Set up five of these unique hook book blogs over a few weeks and look at the great posts you can make on Twitter and Facebook to promote them. If each of those blogs have 500 followers, you've just touched 2,500 people you never would have reached otherwise. It's a win/win.

Seeing blogs differently can open a ton of doors for you and help massively broaden your audience.

Changes for My Blog

REAL-LIFE VISIBILITY—Now let's talk about the real world, outside your door and not on the internet. I know, I know, we writers easily forget about the world outside. The internet is so easy and fun and jeeze, we don't even have to put on decent clothes to sit down and connect. But connection on one more level can only help. Marketing isn't just about doing one or two things, successful marketing requires we overlap and layer audience in as many places and ways possible. This doesn't necessarily mean more work, it just means organizing and scheduling different approaches on various days.

Remember how I suggested that you tweet at different times each day? That's done in an effort to gain a broader exposure to more people on Twitter. If you tweet at the same time every day, you could possibly be talking to the same three people on Twitter every day. I also never suggest that people use social networks during the weekends. Why? It's harder to be seen and heard while all the crazies are out tweeting about which Hollywood star is involved with who, and who's splitting up with who. A marketing author's time is valuable and we need to protect it and only make efforts when it works best.

So, why leave the house? To be seen and heard and visible. If you volunteer in your neighborhood a lot, you're seen. If you're a member of a clean-up committee for your church events, you're seen. If you do a book event for the local gardener's group, you've been visible. If you go to the chamber of commerce meetings, help at local fundraising events or block parties, you are seen. When you're this active, you become someone people go to. People like the press.

What a great newspaper story when you are not only mentioned as someone active in your community, but also the author of the book *Angel Crime Solver*. You don't need to do everything I mentioned, but find things that interest you. Along the way, you may discover cool locations for book events, or wonderful businesses or charities that fit perfectly with your unique hook. Always carry printed flyers with your book cover, book blurb, distribution venues and buy link in your car. Post them where you can, at the grocery store, community, church, or veterinarian's bulletin board. Talk about your book when it easily comes up and be sure to offer a flyer to that person, whether it's a receptionist, check-out person, or waitress.

This isn't a hard-push kind of approach at all. The flyers are available and when the subject comes up, you already have them on you. I know an author who actually carries a case of books in her car for just these occasions. She's sold several of them just over casual conversations. This REAL-LIFE VISIBILITY platform is just that, a platform. Be casual, be happy, be proud of your accomplishment. Keep your eyes peeled for the best opportunities for further marketing and just get out of the house every once in a while! If you do this one afternoon a week, you will be amazed how your marketing outlook shifts. Join a community organization or group. Offer to do book events for appropriate unique hook groups. Talk about your book when someone asks, "What do you do?" Open up your life!

My Real-Life Visibility Plan

CROSS MARKETING CONCEPTS

Cross Marketing may sound like a complicated idea, but it's very simple. It just requires a slight shift in your thinking, like most of the marketing concepts I teach. Cross marketing is another way of finding lovers of your book's unique hooks in different places, and reaching them in different ways. The coolest thing about cross marketing is that the AUDIENCE IS ALREADY GATHERED FOR YOU!

We've already touched slightly on cross marketing when we talked about Facebook Groups and Twitter accounts. If your book is a historical fiction about a poor New York Victorian woman who pulls off a bank robbery and never gets caught, you have a great ©SuperGenre. It might look like this:

Antique lovers, vintage clothing, vintage shoes, hats, corsets, Victorian Era travel, weapons, Victorian houses, etc.

The Facebook groups you might join are groups that love those things and talk about them. On Twitter, you might look for accounts loaded with antique lovers, Victorian weapons collectors, vintage clothing lovers, etc. The followers of those accounts are perfect for your Twitter account.

You have found lovers of your unique hooks in different places and reached out to them in those venues. Facebook and Twitter are just the tip of the iceberg.

Let's imagine for a moment that you can take flight. Lift off and spread your wings and look down at the world. There are a million ways to reach people who love the unique hooks within this particular book.

Over there is the Victorian part of your city and there's always a lot of renovation going on there. People who love old homes are addicted to them, they love buying them, refurbishing them, furnishing them, making them as close to the original as possible, even selling them and starting all over again. In addition to the people who actually do this, are the people who would love to do it but don't. Right there are several directions for powerful cross marketing. Think it through!

- Antique collectors and sellers
- Vintage clothing businesses
- Millwork businesses that make specialty details for this kind for home
- Carpet and window treatment companies
- Victorian homeowner groups
- Victorian house restoration businesses
- Victorian houses turned restaurants
- Victorian house tour organizers
- Real estate companies that specialize in Victorian properties
- Historical societies

And that's just the beginning. Fly further, to some of the resort communities all over the country that are built around Victorian era structures. On the east coast we have Cape May, New Jersey. In New York there's Lake Chautauqua. Some areas of San Diego and almost all of old San Francisco feature Victorian homes, refurbished and beautiful. Nearly every single state and country has their protected Victorian historic area.

Let's fly over other towns and take a look at how obsessed people can get over antiques, vintage clothing, shoes, corsets, guns and we're seeing yet more cross markets.

Grasping the concept of cross marketing requires spreading your creative thinking wings. Anywhere people love your book's unique hook is a possible cross market. This is very different, and far more effective, than the "Buy my book!" approach. Now you can see that prospective book buyers are in far more places than book stores on online book selling locations. They're everywhere.

Before we get in to how to create effecting cross marketing strategies, I'd like you to take flight and look for your book's cross markets.

My Book's Unique Hook Cross Markets

PLATFORM EXPANSION

I totally understand that at this point you might be hyperventilating, but take a deep breath. You've seen that you need to have a regularly updated website, you grasp the power of a unique hook blog with entries every other week, and you understand that you need to build and maintain a unique hook Twitter account, Monday through Friday, and belong to and post on several unique hook Facebook groups Monday through Friday. The mere idea of expanding those platforms might seem overwhelming but that's not at all what I'm saying.

We all know the phrase, "Making money on other people's money." Cross marketing platform expansion is kind of like that. We will be using other people's audience to create more book sales. We'll be using the audiences of all those cool cross markets you listed. Why? Because, these cross markets are already filled with lovers of your unique hooks, and they aren't being bombarded by other authors shouting "Buy my book!"

This is how a great cross marketing effort works. Let's continue with the story about the Victorian woman bank robber. The ©SuperGenre is:

Antique lovers, vintage clothing, vintage shoes, hats, corsets, Victorian Era travel, weapons, houses, etc.

That ©SuperGenre led us to several cross marketing focuses, but let's pick four and show three different ways to cross market for broader market expansion.

- Antique collectors and sellers
    - These are wonderful locations for a book sale and signing event, especially if the location has several antique dealers together in a large place, like an Antique Village or Antique Warehouse. Contact the owner, arrange for a meeting and discuss the connection between your book and the wonderful antiques. Make this a win/win. Tell the owner that you'll be promoting the event to your networks and bringing in customers for the dealers. At the same time, your table will get the opportunity to take advantage of the antique lovers attending.
- Vintage clothing businesses
    - Remember, these cross markets can work on line, too. Google vintage clothing businesses. They all have a website. Locate the contact information for the owner of the business. If that's not easy to find, simply contact the webmaster and they will connect you. Once you've made contact, make your proposal. Again, this has to be a win/win or there's no motivation for them to participate. Propose that you would like to write a 750-word article once each month that holds interesting facts about Victorian clothing, fabrics, fashion, and style. You will explore

women's shoes, coats, blouses, corsets, underthings, and night clothes. You'll talk about men's suits, shoes, leisure wear, underwear, etc. Your small pieces will be entertaining and informative and you will write them for the company's website at no charge *PROVIDING* they permit you to include your book title, buy link, and book cover for each month's piece. You can even end each piece with a quiz about coming topics. This should be fun and entertaining for you, your unique hook lovers on the company's website, and the company. What you're doing is giving him entertaining web content in return for a shot at promoting your book to his already established customer base. It's a once a month effort that can expose you to hundreds of new prospective book buyers who already love your unique hooks. This approach works for any business related to your unique hooks, including Victorian house restoration businesses, and real estate companies featuring Victorian properties. Carefully design your proposal for the best impact for both you and the business.

- Victorian house owner groups
    - Speaking engagements are powerful with these kinds of groups. You speak about the era, what inspired you to write the story, how much research you did, and how much you love the

Victorian era. Then you would do a reading and a book sale and signing. This also works well for Historical Societies. Groups like this are always looking for interesting speakers

Now. Let's take a new look at the numbers. While other authors are shouting together in the same places, you've expanded your audience into unique hook Facebook Groups (eventually as many as 60 groups), built your Twitter account with thousands of unique hook lovers, blog about your unique hooks to your hundreds of unique hook blog followers, reached out to bloggers who focus on your unique hooks, guest blogged, and collected another several-thousand exposures for you and your book. And now, you've taken advantage of cross markets and their audiences that could collect another several thousand between online business websites and live speaking engagements. Other authors are struggling to get people to buy their book, while you are simply connecting with people who love what's inside your book—a LOT MORE PEOPLE, too.

My Cross Marketing Directions and Proposals

MULTI-LEVEL MARKETING

We all know what multi-tasking is. It's when we do several things at the same time, however, it works best when there's a plan. Multi-level marketing needs a schedule and a plan, it needs commitment and creativity. And, it can't be developed over night.

Most authors have two goals in mind:

1. Get that marketing thing finished
2. Write the next book.

Number one, marketing must be approached with enthusiasm and creativity to assure its success. And number two, time to write your next book must be protected at all cost. But always remember, without sales and loyal fans, what's the point of writing the next book? It's time to see writing and marketing as two parts of the same wheel. The spokes are everything you do to bring sales, collect loyal fans, and protect time to write.

Authors look at marketing as a hateful task that should be over with as soon as possible. They Facebook and tweet then brush off their hands and forget it. They did what they had to do, so where are all the sales? Think about it. If you only cook hot dogs for your family's dinner every single day, they get bored with hot dogs. Eventually they don't even show up at the table. It's the same with marketing.

Attaining real marketing success requires understanding that this is a creative process. It should be as much fun as writing the book you're trying to market, and it should be approached professionally and with respect. Doing this on multiple levels is how serious marketing gets serious results. Think about all the marketing going on in the world around us.

Does Coke only market their cola at the point of purchase with the logo on the soda machine or cooler door? They do not. Coke extrapolates their unique hooks as far as possible. The unique hooks for Coca-Cola are family, youth, fun, picnics, holidays, hard work, taking a break, enjoying great music, etc. This is why every single time you see a bottle of Coke it's connected to one of those unique hooks—a commercial of high school kids on their first day of classes, a mom taking a break while the new baby sleeps, a businessman leaning back in his car after a great meeting and enjoying a Coke, a family sipping Coke at the lake or the slopes or around the Christmas tree. These are television commercials, radio ads, newspaper ads, billboards, bus signage, grocery store flyers, convenience store windows, and so much more. In addition to all that, Coca-Cola sponsors sporting and entertainment events. That's multi-level marketing. It touches many of the product's unique hooks, speaks to many different audiences, and reached them in many different ways and places. That's how real marketing works.

Granted, your book is not Coca-Cola, but it deserves the same strategy. Once you build your unique hook Facebook Groups membership and unique hook Twitter following, you've only just begun. The next steps are to develop your book's ©SuperGenre and locate audiences, then to stretch your cross-marketing muscles and locate all the places and ways you can reach more and more of those people.

There are online venues and live venues, businesses and organizations, charities and broad stroke connections to make all over the place in so many ways. You can create unique hook Facebook groups of your own, you can develop wonderful storytelling strategies with Pinterest that can promote sales, you can create your own YouTube channels to explore the unique hooks and bring lovers of those things closer to your sales link. You can create a plan that gives you flexibility and power at the same time.

And the biggest reward of all is when you start seeing a marked climb in sales. That encourages you to charge ahead and make more things happen, connect with more unique hook lovers in more places. It's a high all authors deserve, the joy of selling a lot of books! While your competition sits stagnant, doing the same thing every day, you're making real progress because you're doing actual, real marketing and creating connections.

READY FOR THE COOLEST PART OF ALL?

The first, the MOST IMPORTANT thing to do is COMMIT TO NO MORE OR LESS THAN <u>ONE HOUR A DAY</u> for marketing. I can hear you already. It takes you hours and hours to post on your social networks. I know why it takes you so long—because you're not marketing, you're socializing. Social media is a marketing tool, and until you see it as such, you can't grasp the best ways to use it. If you spend time socializing, it's not selling books, it's making buddies and being social. That's not your marketing time, it's your social time and you must keep them separate. Better yet, eliminate the socializing time altogether. It isn't serving you, it's eating up your writing time.

Now within that one hour a day, you can do a number of different things, so you'll need to schedule activities carefully. Every weekday, from Monday through Friday you will:

- Twitter for ten minutes in the morning and ten minutes in the afternoon, PLUS five minutes to follow more unique hook lovers. This totals 30 minutes on Twitter. Those ten tweets might include:
  o Promote a guest blog at a unique hook blogger's blog (with link)
  o Post a value-added article about one of your unique hooks found on Google Alerts (with link)
  o Promote your own unique hook blog entry from weeks ago (with link)
  o Post pictures of a unique hook item (with link to your blog or website)
  o Post the link to your website activities page "Look what I'm up to!"

- Post your book link and the book cover art
- Post the newest link to your newest unique hook blog entry
- Link to your Pinterest loaded with unique hook pics
- Post a link to a unique hook business website that has your articles
- Post a link to your unique hook YouTube channel

- Post on ten Facebook Groups in the morning and ten unique hook Facebook Groups in the afternoon. This should total 20 minutes on Facebook. Those posts might be any one of these:
  - Link to your newest blog entry
  - Link to a unique hook business where you have articles
  - Link to guest blog for unique hook blogger
  - Link to your website's activities page
  - Pics of your unique hooks with links to your blog or website
  - Links to your unique hook YouTube channel
  - Link to your Pinterest loaded with unique hook items

So, with 30 minutes a day committed to Twitter from Monday through Friday, and 20 minutes a day committed to Facebook from Monday through Friday, that leaves you 10 minutes a day, Monday through Friday, for marketing. Those ten minutes could be filled with seeking out new unique hook cross markets, locating unique hook guest blog opportunities, exploring local unique hook clubs and organizations for speaking engagements. Your choice.

Now let's talk about the weekend. Those two days also require one hour each for marketing, however it will not be on social networks. Those two hours will serve you well for writing cross marketing events proposals, and writing guest blogs (remember, every unique hook guest blog must have original content.) You can develop charity events, write several of your own unique hook blog entries to get ahead of the game, or even step outside and pass out your flyers while stopping at the dry cleaners, grocery store, or dentist. It's your choice. You know when a unique hook website article is due so schedule writing it on the weekend. You know when you have a speaking engagement so prepare your handouts. You know when you are holding a book event, so pack up your books, table cloth, decorations, or whatever you do to make your table inviting.

Plan your work and ALWAYS keep an eye on the clock. If it takes you longer to write a blog or an article than the time allotted, then limit your cross-marketing activities until you have a stock pile of those blog entries and articles written. I like to write my tweets and Facebook posts for the week on the weekend. I type them all on a word doc (along with the links) then just copy/paste, Monday through Friday. I've had author clients tell me that they build their Twitter following on their cell phone while watching the football games on Sundays. Whatever works for you. If you use the weekend two hours to plan and prepare well, and it only takes you one hour a day, Monday through Friday to market, that leaves you a LOT of hours a day to write. That success wheel can keep on rolling.

MARKETING TIME MANAGEMENT

There are no tricks to finishing tasks and being successful. It's all about making a plan and following it faithfully. Marketing is not a game or a distraction, it's part of the successful author's job. Commitment is the key to success and making a workable plan is extremely important. The one-hour a day/seven hours a week plan works well for most authors, however there are a few who work faster, and some who work much slower. If you want and need to spend two hours a day, go for it. This has to fit around you and your life.

One hour a day may means that you can't build in your cross-marketing efforts right away, and that's fine. It might mean that you pull those extra 50 minutes of extra time from the weekdays to add to your weekend work. It may mean that you pick and choose what you work on more carefully. Either way, it will only work if it works for YOU.

Don't overwhelm yourself. Start simple then add cross marketing and live event efforts as you perfect and shave minutes off your daily activities. Everything gets easier with time and practice and if you want real success, you'll need to take as much time and practice as you need to get there. For some of you, this will be a piece of cake. No matter how busy your life is, one hour a day to improve your book sales is worth it.

Here's an example of a time management chart that works for the author:

MARKETING TIME MANAGEMENT CHART
MONDAY - FRIDAY MARKETING SCHEDULE

Twitter
9:10 AM – 9:25 AM

Promo Tweets	*10*
Retweets/Thank yous	*3*
Build following	*Followed 20 new unique hook lovers*

4:40 PM – 4:55 PM

Promo Tweets	*10*
Retweets /Thank yous	*4*
Build following	*Followed 34 new unique hook lovers*
Total Time Spent	***30 minutes***

Facebook Groups

Promo Posts	*Post to 10 FB groups in the morning*
Promo Posts	*Post to 10 FB groups in the afternoon*
Search New	*Joined 2 new FB unique hook groups*
Total Time Spent	***20 minutes***

Targeted Networking

Research	*Unique hook bloggers for guest blog tour*
Total Time Spent	***10 minutes***

M- F DAILY TOTAL	**60 MINUTES PER DAY**

WEEKEND MARKETING SCHEDULE
Creative Development

Write Tweets for the week	*20 minutes*
Write Facebook posts for the week	*10 minutes*
Write next guest blog entry	*30 minutes*
Prepare for Saturday speaking event	*15 minutes*
Research new unique hook speaking groups	*15 minutes*
Work on YouTube channel entry	*30 minutes*

WEEKEND TOTAL   **120 MINUTES TOTAL**

That's all it is. A plan. A strategy. An effective schedule of activity that keeps you and your book visible. At first, you'll struggle with fitting everything into the time scheduled, but it gets easier and you will find ways to streamline your work. You can pre-post and schedule blogs, so when working on your unique hook blog entries, consider developing four or five blogs in a series and writing them all at one time. Then you can post them and schedule them for your release date. CAUTION: Remember to always check those blogs, because sometimes when they go live, the pictures might not appear. It might take a little time to get the system working for you. I use WordPress because of the wonderful SEO. I seldom have issues with blog entries going live without the pics or in need of tweaking, but I always check.

Twitter, too has a few shortcuts but I STRONGLY SUGGEST that you don't use them. Because Twitter moves so quickly in a live stream, it's important to be present when you're on Twitter. It's only fifteen minutes in the morning and fifteen minutes in the afternoon. It's a break from writing, too.

Facebook has a few little idiosyncrasies. Facebook does not like anything that seems to too systemized. If Facebook thinks you're spamming, punishment will come swiftly and without warning. You'll get banned from groups and all your posts to those groups will be deleted. It's nasty. That's why I suggest posting on ten different Facebook unique hook groups at a time.

Post on Facebook groups 1-10 on Tuesday morning. Post on Facebook groups 11-20 on Tuesday afternoon. Post on Facebook groups 21-30 on Thursday morning. Post on Facebook groups 31-40 on Thursday afternoon. If you have sixty or more groups, post on Wednesdays, too.

Those two weekend hours are extremely valuable as they are your planning time. During that time, you will prepare everything so that Monday through Friday can skim by at an hour a day, and you can focus on your writing projects.

Now it's time to create your own schedule.

My Marketing Time Management Chart

AUTHOR BIO

Deborah Riley-Magnus is an author and an Author Success Coach. She has a twenty-seven-year professional background in marketing, advertising, and public relations and has been a writer for print, television, and radio. Her nonfiction—FINDING AUTHOR SUCCESS, CROSS MARKETING MAGIC FOR AUTHORS, and the newest, WRITE BRAIN/LEFT BRAIN— focuses on helping authors by teaching them how to bridge the gap between the creative writer and the marketing author. As an Author Success Coach she produces several pieces monthly for various websites and online publications. She teaches online and live workshops, clinics, and boot camps. She writes an author marketing industry blog and coaches authors, one-on-one, for sales success. She belongs to several writing and professional organizations.

In addition to writing nonfiction marketing books for authors, Deborah also writes fiction. She has lived on both the east and west coast of the United States and has traveled the country widely. She is a native of Pittsburgh, Pennsylvania and recently returned after living in Los Angeles, California for several years.

Blog - http://rileymagnus.wordpress.com/
Teach - http://theauthorsuccesscoach.com/
Fiction – http://drmagnusfantasy.com/
Tweet – http://twitter.com/rileymagnus
Facebook - http://www.facebook.com/deborah.rileymagnus
LinkedIn -https://www.linkedin.com/in/deborah-riley-magnus-4ba15a1a/

AUTHOR MARKETING PLAYBOOKS
by Deborah Riley-Magnus

AUTHOR MARKETING PLAYBOOK #1
*Using Your Words for Marketing,
Hooking the RIGHT Book Buyers,
and Growing Audience*

AUTHOR MARKETING PLAYBOOK #2
*Understanding the Charity Effect,
Being Socially Networked
And Keeping Your Marketing Momentum Alive*

AUTHOR MARKETING PLAYBOOK #3
*Taking control by Writing for the Market,
Using Hand-in Hand Writing and Marketing Techniques,
Implementing Advanced Marketing Strategies*

AUTHOR MARKETING BOOKS
by Deborah Riley-Magnus

WRITE BRAIN LEFT BRAIN:
Bridging the Gap Between Creative Writer and Marketing Author

CROSS MARKETING MAGIC FOR AUTHORS:
Developing New Avenues for Advanced Book Marketing

FINDING AUTHOR SUCCESS:
Discovering and Uncovering the Marketing Power Within your Manuscript

www.ingramcontent.com/pod-product-compliance
Lightning Source LLC
Chambersburg PA
CBHW082331220526
45470CB00008B/2468